Poems on the Precipice

Poems on the Precipice

by

Elise Chadwick

© 2025 Elise Chadwick. All rights reserved.
This material may not be reproduced in any form, published,
reprinted, recorded, performed, broadcast,
rewritten, or redistributed without
the explicit permission of Elise Chadwick.
All such actions are strictly prohibited by law.

Cover design by Shay Culligan
Cover image by Point Normal on Unsplash
Author image by B. Docktor

ISBN: 978-1-63980-890-8

Kelsay Books
502 South 1040 East, A-119
American Fork, Utah 84003
Kelsaybooks.com

for Michael,
my first reader and life-long champion

and for my boys,
Max and Ben

Acknowledgments

I'd like to thank these journals for publishing the following poems:

The Avenue: "Making Room"
The Elevation Review: "Lunch at Bob's, 1965"
Gyroscope: "Her Suffering"
Inkwell Journal: "Uphill"
Inscape: "Cutting Class"
The Listening Eye: "Memory Care," "Desperately Seeking," "Black Hole"
Literary Mama: "Henry's Song"
Muddy River Poetry Review: "English Class, 1985"
Naugatuck Review: "Overwound"
Paterson Literary Review: "This Is a Body"
Still Point Arts Quarterly: "May 28, 2019"
US1 Worksheets: "Hiding in Plain Sight"

Contents

INNOCENCE

Hiding in Plain Sight	15
This Is a Body	16
Henry's Song	18
All you do is sit in a chair all day and listen to people talk	20
Reflections at the Museum of Natural History	22
Pockets of Generosity	23
Almost 10	24
Lunch at Bob's, 1965	26
Quarantined, Summer 1968	28
English Class, 1985	30
Cutting Class	32
The Collector	34
Promise of Beauty	36

EXPERIENCE

I Couldn't See This Coming	41
Overwound	42
In the Waiting Room	44
Her Suffering	47
Black Hole	49
Desperately Seeking	50
Memory Care	52
Making Room	54
Uphill	55
May 28, 2019	57
Ash Friday	59
In My Next Life	61

It's only on the brink that people find the will to change. Only at the precipice do we evolve.
—John Cleese

*Mind led body
to the edge of the precipice.
They stared in desire
at the naked abyss.
If you love me, said mind,
take that step into silence.
If you love me, said body,
turn and exist.*
—Anne Stevenson

INNOCENCE

Hiding in Plain Sight

Days after
the first Monday
in September, class
rosters and seating charts
crisp with promise, I divine your
presence before two test lines confirm
it. Internal twinges and tenderness. Irritability.
Nausea. Textbook signs I keep to myself. Early days,
I pace locker lined halls or sit at my desk planning lessons,
your burgeoning cloaked in the loose drape of my blouse.
Soft swell hidden beneath books and bags slung belly up.
Tucked under the Formica lip of my desk. Mid-semester,
sideways standing in front of the room, one eye on the
chalkboard, the other on the class clown, I startle at the
flutter. Foreign. Familiar. A black-eyed butterflyfish
afloat. Before April blooms you somersault in your
bubble of amniotic fluid. I admire the ripple of
your dance, outstretched arm or bent leg,
across the buddha belly expanse. Concealed
still but the secret no longer ours. At night
I dream of a tidy delivery, a symbiotic
labor during prep period. I tuck you
into a rattly metal file cabinet
drawer safe among stacks
of lesson plans where
you snooze until the
final bell rings.

This Is a Body

an ode to Sally

It's been a long afternoon
of bubble blowing, chalk art
and racing in the pool.
We are soggy and puckered,
the soles of our feet scorched
from our sprint on the porch floor.

In the bathroom, still dripping,
we peel off our suits,
mine, faded and baggy
where the elastic has started to dissolve,
hers, green and vibrant,
sequined butterfly sparkling on her chest.
We step into the shower together.

Her seven-year-old body is lean and strong,
her olive skin unblemished by sun or time
except for the tiny mole we call a beauty mark
barely visible on her left butt cheek
and there is not even a whisper of
self-consciousness for this body
that has never been
shamed or humiliated
let down or deceived
threatened or violated
trampled or broken
cut open or stitched up
ignored as if invisible or
told it's ugly or too fat.

This is a body
pristine and pure
that measures itself only
against faint pencil marks
scratched on a door frame.

This is a body that wakens
with laughter and unseen dreams
that have a future.

This is a body that every day
jumps higher, hangs longer
and zooms faster, believing
that helmets and knee pads,
are the only protection it needs.

Henry's Song

He knows Peter's theme by heart
and hums it to himself when
he builds cardboard skyscrapers or
weaves webs of yarn round doorknobs
and kitchen drawer handles.

The melody of the strings
summons plaid school satchels
abandoned for tree climbing,
romping through bright fields
immune to the danger
of plain old grey wolves or
the colorful fairytale ones
thinly tucked into bonnets and aprons
lurking in doorways or
tumbling down red brick fireplaces
blazing with flames.

Sitting side by side
on the red damask sofa
he sucks his calloused thumb
and caresses his threadbare doggie
keeping time with the music,
listening beyond the crackle and burp,
as the needle steers its way across
the grooves in the ancient black vinyl
past the slinking of the clarinet cat
and the flute bird fluttering.

When the mellow brass of the French horns
signals the presence
of the skulking saw-toothed wolf,
we see his shadowy paw prints
in the snowy woods,
and the thumb sucking slows
now more distraction
than comfort.
Even though we know it's just a trick
and that she is resting safely
in the hollow of the tree
we mourn Sonja swallowed whole
into the dark
of the wolf's belly.

And even though we know it's a happy ending
for Peter who traps that wolf with a rope
wound round its bushy tail
when I tuck him into bed that night
into the darkness he asks
a simmering not so simple question—
*but the wolf isn't real,
right?*

All you do is sit in a chair all day and listen to people talk

I know what you're thinking.
Three years of fun and games at *Little Blessings*
where Miss Jean's brilliance sparkles
over the wellspring of her patience.
Even more years watching his big sister
board the bus and disappear down the dark aisle
only to return at day's end with a bounce
in her ponytail. He's five years old
and it's time for kindergarten.

You can hardly contain your excitement.
So much independence coming his way.
Climb the steep bus steps. Find a seat.
Clasp the seatbelt. Carry a big boy
backpack weighted with the lunch
& snack Mommy prepared the night
before. But your excitement
is not contagious. And he's not
fooled by it either.

He understands what he's leaving behind:
early morning lounging in his pj's
dreamy thumb sucking with *Doggy*
dawdling over soggy bowls of *Lucky Charms*
surprise of grocery shopping treats
library roaming and mountains
of books on sharks and dinosaurs
dirty kneed playground climbing
catnaps on the living room carpet
bathed in the shadow of afternoon light.

It's been a week now
since kindergarten started.
I watch him at the bus stop
climbing those steps. Dutiful soldier,
backpack full of resignation.
Ask him how he likes it and see
if your heart doesn't break
when he tells you the truth.

Reflections at the Museum of Natural History

We go for the sharks, queue impatience,
to watch those apex predators, great whites,
and more. They mesmerize in their watery
underworld, jagged smiles welcoming as prison
grates in search of calories enough to fill
from sifted plankton and krill.
Sleepless lidless eyes. Torpedoes forever
on the move like the five-year-old boy
on the other side of the glass still
part feral though civilized too.

But we stay for the *Hall of Human Origins*
hypnotized by the Neanderthal family
reconstructed, scantily clad and stocky.
Posed photo shoot close, glassy eyes
cast their own spell and bewitch
the boy to join them on their journey
back through the primeval forest
to the warmth of a cave hearth ablaze.

Pockets of Generosity

Remember the first time we walked city blocks.
Whirr of tires on pavement. Musical beat bleats
of ambulances gaining on us from behind.
Snort of accordion pleated buses pulling away
from stops. You had learned to count past ten
and practiced on a parade of yellow taxis.

You were used to the absence of sidewalks
and cars. Walking to the crunch of gravel and
bird chatter, with time to kick stones, pick
wildflowers and feed donkeys the carrots stowed
in your pockets. You were used to measuring
last night's rain by the running of the creek.

I remember the first time we walked city blocks.
How we approached the man, lost in layers
of loose dirty clothing, sprawled on the pavement,
flanked by torn black garbage bags. Others
sidestepped and looked away.

Though you could not read his cardboard
plea, you understood. I remember you
reached deep into your pocket and found
your treasure from the tooth fairy and gave it
to the man.

Almost 10

After years of baby steps—
solo ventures across the street for playdates,
walks home from the bus stop, bike rides
to the dead end—they hold hands when
they walk, one blonde and bespectacled,
wearing her brother's hand-me-down
hi-tops and a denim jacket. The other
delicate and dark in bold leggings
and perky print hoodie.

They've travelled the route hundreds
of times. Red-cheeked passengers
in strollers graduating to wobbling
and toddling. Runners and climbers
testing limits. Today, freedom tickles
their noses and fills their lungs.

They dodge sidewalk cracks. Sidestep
oily puddles that glisten beneath the
rumbling overpass. Admire the graffiti
and look to see if there's anything new.
Pass the bank to the crosswalk. Mournful
train whistle signals almost there. Cars slow
then stop at crosswalks.

Their destination is *Mimi's*. Lattes and vegan
gluten-free pastry offerings printed in pastel
on a chalkboard. The girls know their order
before they approach the counter. They count
out their money, pocket the change and sit
in a corner. When their avocado toast
and Nutella pancakes arrive, they pause.
No longer hungry. Their craving
has already been satisfied.

Lunch at Bob's, 1965

When the lunch bell rings
we rush from stuffy classrooms,
stampede through hallways
that smell of polish and disinfectant
tumble in a jumble down
the double wide staircase,
smooth wood banister daring
anyone willing to risk the ire
of Mr. Salinger standing guard.

Hungry for sun and lunch
most run to mothers
gossiping in shirt sleeves
ready to ferry their charges home
before returning them to school
for the afternoon session.

The walkers, who live close enough
and have permission,
chatter with the frenzy of the newly sprung,
as they make their way home
to apron-clad mothers
ready to serve them lunch
when they breach the front door.

I find my sisters by the flagpole,
our designated meeting spot
brown bags in hand.
We walk together up the hill
past the castle shaped Episcopal Church
with its seasonal display of fake sheep
and creepy cradle-laden baby Jesus

past the open door of Donatello's
where wafting clouds of hairspray and cigarette smoke
make us gag just a little bit when we walk by,
past the circular stone staircase that leads down to the-warren
where Tony, the shoe repair man sits
buried among heaps of leather
banging and stitching and stretching.

Finally, we arrive at Bob's.
Balding and soft faced,
apron smeared with chocolate ice-cream smudges
wrapped around the beginnings of a paunch.
He's endlessly patient with neighborhood children
mesmerized by this hole in the wall suburban dime-store
its glass candy counter cloudy with sticky fingerprints
squeaky metal racks of comic books and *Mad* Magazines,
every nook and cranny of the store filled
with undiscovered treasure.

From behind the soda fountain counter, he smiles.
Mother works at the art gallery in town today
and he's been expecting us.
We plunk down three in a row
on the red leather stools that twirl
and are too high up for our feet to touch the ground.
What'll it be girls? he asks.

Quarantined, Summer 1968

I mostly remember sweltering
sequestration in the airless attic,
one sealed window overlooking
tetherball, paralyzing boredom
and the unrelenting itch.

On the long bus ride to Maine,
some renewed friendships.
Others sat in quiet isolation.
My seatmate shared with me
her case of the chicken pox.

Of course, Mother sent a package
wrapped in brown paper, addressed
in *Palmer* method cursive, stuffed
with *Mad Libs* and comic books,
Veronica and Archie.
Calamine too, useless except
to stain pink my bed sheets and pj's.

Up the creaking staircase, gray meals
on trays ascended, wobbly and perspiring.
The chant of communal prayer,
clang of silverware and scrape of chairs,
a crescendo of laughter and song rose
through floorboards during mealtime.

Waiting for the rash of pus-filled blisters
to burst, crust and scab, mad
to resist the itch to scratch
for fear of permanent scarring,
days and nights blurred.

When all was silent in the dim attic,
I found myself longing for things
I hated most about camp. Early
morning dives off the splintered
dock into frigid Lake Pequaket,
maniacally treading water, evading
bloodsuckers that colonized the dock.

Now, I pictured Hutch,
hulk of a horse whose jerky
snorting and fly swatting tail
terrorized me daily, and imagined
myself astride his haunches
parading around the dusty ring.

I even missed the scratch of
my green wool blanket,
the stiff white sheet and dreamed
of returning to my cabin. There
I would sleep comfortably curled
on my tidy cot.

Finally, one ordinary summer day
the nurse declared me no longer contagious.
Penitent liberated from Plato's cave,
I shielded my eyes and descended
the attic stairs awakened.

English Class, 1985

He sat in the back row next to
the broken window, the one
for which I sent a weekly work order
fearing the guillotine decapitation
of a class clown trying to climb out
the window for a few laughs.

He observed his classmates from this post,
a quiet presence, a rare participant.
He sized me up, too.

With the arrogance of the newly minted
teacher, I thought I knew him, thought
I recognized his type. Unobtrusive,
conscientious, respected by his peers,
handsome in a wholesome preppy way.
Destined for an ivy—or one tier down.
Non aggressively athletic, tennis
or squash or golf. Periodic head swing
lifting the sheaf of thick brown hair
from his eyes so that ours could meet
when I returned papers to him
or he asked for an extension—
family problems he'd explain.

He was nothing like the attention seeking
football players who over-stuffed
the front row, leather sleeved letter
jackets sprawled over the backs
of their chairs. They raised their hands
even though they hadn't read the book,
had nothing much to say but needed
to be noticed by everyone in the room.

It was early May when students and
teachers alike can taste the stretch
of freedom ahead. We'd just returned
from a fire drill where we gathered
in the parking lot awaiting the principal's
voice over the loudspeaker. This was
decades before cell phones, lockdown
drills and active shooters on campus.

With 15 minutes left on the clock
we returned to the classroom, a still life
of abandoned books and scattered backpacks,
chairs untucked from their desks, scribbles
on a chalkboard memorializing a conversation
that had just begun to gain momentum.

So, what does the color purple mean,
I ask, *not only in our ordinary life
but here in this book?*

Debate re-ignites. Sparks of smug
certainty. Skepticism smolders.
A question challenges. *How do you know
that the color purple relates to being gay?*
someone challenges.

Just as the bell rings
imposing an end to our discussion
he rises from the back row. In a voice
I barely recognize he declares *I know
because I'm gay* and strolls out of the room.

Cutting Class

for Chiara

We're sandwiched between
the dusty chalkboard
and the black magic wardrobe
filled to overflow with
course outlines, vocabulary lists,
broken paper backs and stacks
of razor edged manilla folders
stuffed with essential questions.
Side by side at the computer table
teetering on wobbly plastic chairs
mug of coffee long cold,
we're invisible to passersby in the hall.

Was it chance that charted her daily
pilgrimage past my classroom
during prep period?
Lingering doorway hellos evolved
to stilted standing chatter
about immigrant grandparents
and twin siblings,
thin athletic academic stars,
popular perfection incarnate,
everything she believed she was not.

Weeks passed before I invited her
to sit at the cloistered desk
with me uncertain of her desire
to disclose her perfect contrition.
With chipped polished fingers curled
around the hem of her sleeve, she tugged
upward 'til the gauzy folds of her blouse
nestled in the crook of her elbow revealed,
neatly spaced as railroad ties,
the sorrow of her soul.

The Collector

The attachments start in pre-school.
Heart-tagged *Beanie Babies*. Baboo & Lola,
patchwork panda and rainbow llama,
squish and sigh in his embrace.

In middle school it is the rubber
band ball. Sphere of kinetic energy.
Part science experiment. Part compulsion.
Bands filched from junk drawers and
doorknobs, stretched by the colorful
hundreds. Heavy as an anvil.
It disintegrates in the dry heat
of the attic exile.

And then come *Marvel Superhero*
and *Magic the Gathering*. Promises
of invincibility stacked in teetering piles
or displayed singly in cloudy page protectors.
Boxes of them purchased at the bodega
down the hill. The climb back up an eternity
of impatience for rare enchantment and sorcery
in foil-wrapped packs.

In high school, big bellied buddhas
made of faux jade and bronze meditate
and laugh, inspiring spiritual curiosity
before accumulating the dust of rejection.
They remind us of a nickname lost
from when he, too, was round and soft.

Now he's enchanted by non-fungible tokens
magically mined sorcery stored in the blockchain
and invincible digital wallets, his spirit
most animated in the ether of Ethereum.

Promise of Beauty

We study the moon-faced clock.
Looming numerals chart
the arrival of the 6:18.
We train our eyes on the stairs.

Headlight down the track.
A whistle then a rattle on the rails.
The train materializes
in a puff of steam.

The strain of the work week drains
with each step toward the car.
Click of the door handle. He climbs
into the back with Sally.

*Do you remember when we played
pretend sleeping and you snored
really loud?* she squeals,
ready to resume their game,

Chatter from the back seat,
melodic and sweet, questions
and nonsensical responses,
waffle, quaffle, bedoffle.

At home, Sally kicks off her sneakers,
runs down the hall and climbs on her bed,
navigating the bed rail with ease
and starts wooing, *Grandpa . . .*

After a brief pause
her calls escalate,
alarming and urgent,
until Grandpa comes.

Maybe his jacket is still on.
Surely he's wearing his shoes,
feet dangling, a giant in a nest
of stuffed animals and blankets.

From the living room, giggles
intersperse with Sally's voice.
Player, director, boss
jumble into one.

Light drains from the room.
Grandpa is reading. No doubt
he's forgotten his glasses.
A hush settles.

I peer out the dark window,
recall the forecast and await
the beauty and light
of the supermoon.

EXPERIENCE

I Couldn't See This Coming

See the speckled mist suspended
over the orb's yellow stain
an ophthalmoscopic snapshot
of a cratered cornea's landscape.

If only the death of limbal stem cells
left a wake of embers, this nose that sniffs out
beach damp in bedsheets and the splash
of coconut on a straphanger wrist
could have detected their demise.

If their exodus made a racket,
or even a quiet hush, these ears that perk
to the whisper of secret heartbeats
and the murmur of silent footsteps
could have stirred to the rustle
of their passing.

I squint to bring my future into focus,
navigating life's dark shadows
foraging nose and ear to the ground
alert to the presence of predators
composing a song of echolocation
and, like the rhinoceros, sometimes
mistaking trees for people
and not minding the conversation.

Overwound

After two desperate months of masked
bedside vigil, watching daylight descend
to dark, inhaling bowls of *Cheerios* and
battling insomnia at home, network tv
commercial breaks marking time until
visiting hours at Columbia Memorial
resume, I schedule the appointment
at Sutton Clock on impulse.

The bare faced black oak 8-day Mission
clock sat for years on our mantle.
Stately, still and quiet, gonging only
when jostled during sporadic dusting.
Brass hinges and gilt Arabic numerals
lonely ornamentation on the sturdy
no nonsense turn of the century time piece.
I can't remember from which downsizing
we inherited it, or if it worked at the time.

Perhaps I am hoping to jump start
time, to apply defibrillator paddles
to this stalled existence or float
free of the quicksand limbo, past
those long weeks between Thanksgiving
and MLK Day when everything
was suspended in non-animation.

I carry the clock to the shop on 82nd,
down a flight of stone stairs where the locked
door warns "by appointment only."
A small lithe man, cottony puffs of hair
framing his face, ushers me into
the heart of the warren. Walls and floors
tick and tock. Without even a glance
at the clock he asks how long it has been
since it ran and I think he is talking
about my own heart beating.

In the Waiting Room

after Elizabeth Bishop

I go alone and wait
for the nurse to call my name.
It is fall. The leaves are beginning
to turn. The elevator is crowded
and there is a line to check in.

The waiting room is full
of walkers and wigs
and walls of abstraction.
And while I wait I study
a pamphlet
then watch the woman
in the head scarf,
weepy blisters,
on forehead and cheeks.
A couple so young
I dream they are lost,
whispering eyes
lowered to phone screens.
A wispy white-haired woman
frail with tremors,
bulky wheelchair attendant
by her side.

I look and look away.

Then, through the door
comes the call,
nurse in white coat,
record sheet on clipboard—

Yes! Here!
It is me
my voice in my mouth.
The nurse guides me
through a sterile maze.
Whirring machines glisten
in fractured daylight.
Everything off below the waist
she commands
and wait
on a paper-sheathed table
that crinkles beneath my weight
for the doctor
who enters quietly and instructs
scoot down
before pressing soft fingers
on my flesh,
navigating his way around
the thing he made.

And the sensation of disconnection
from the round, turning world
dizzies me when I peek
at the raised red thread,
snaking downward
from navel to pubic bone
tidy parallel punctures stapled
on either side of this body
I no longer trust.

How did I come to be here?
When did mutant cells arrive,
divide and migrate,
occupy then colonize?

They assure me
the invaders have been excised.
I suspect there are others
lying in wait.

How many more days
will I find myself here,
among the sick and the dying,
the resigned and the stoic,
patiently waiting
in the waiting room?

Her Suffering

> *how well they understood its human position*
> —W. H. Auden, *Musee des Beaux Arts*

As much as the old masters knew
she knows more
about the solitude of suffering,
the way it encases you like a corset
ivory fingered whale bones pinching
'til the waspwaisted cincture
renders you breathless.

Pale and rail thin
except for the midline coil
of her feeding tube
auburn sweater a smidge darker
than her red hair
part halo, part Goldilocks, still
she knows how to make an entrance.

We visit on lawn chairs
talking through labored speech
and a syringe of pain meds
about books and Netflix and current events
until she commands
with the laser focus
of a wild thing
tell me what's going on with you
and doesn't break the spell until
the litany has been invoked.

A master of misdirection
sleight of hand
and diversions so smooth
it is only hours later
in the looping playback of my mind
that I mourn my failure
to bend the beam inward
and illuminate the pulse
of her suffering.

Black Hole

It's been more than a year since I journeyed
away from myself. This unplanned trip required
no passport or reservation. Has no itinerary.
Open-ended descent. Free fall across familiar
landscapes newly dotted with landmines and craters—
emails punctuated with smiley face emojis,
voice mails just checking to see how I am doing,
invitation— no pressure or rsvp necessary.

Here, the softest sweater, flannel bedsheets
and lambswool socks burn like a throng
of needles on fire.

Let me welcome damp November's invitation
for deep hibernation in the belly of its short
gray days. Let me dream away the winter solstice
in numb oblivion, immune to the promise of
the new year. Leave me in peace to await
the arrival of the vernal equinox before
embarking on the interior pilgrimage back
to myself.

Desperately Seeking

I've never crafted a perky profile or navigated on-line dating sites so when it comes to wading through reams of profiles on the *Psychology Today* directory, it's hard to know when to swipe right.

I type in my zip code, filter for gender and age, and insurance accepted. Scroll to scan the column of faces, heads lilting in poses of casual invitation meets readiness to listen. Skim the openings of blurbs: *I believe, Together we can* and *At the heart of my work.*

Each click tumbles me deeper into a whirling funnel, links to pages papered with credentials, client focus and treatment approaches.
What do I want? What do I need? Mindfulness coaching? Interpersonal, psychodynamic biofeedback? Aren't all therapists emotionally focused, culturally sensitive, and humanistic?

And who knew there could be so many niche issues beyond my run of the mill anxiety and depression? Video game or internet addiction. Hoarding and chronic impulsivity. Is play therapy for adults? I keep clicking.

The attraction is immediate. Soft closed-mouth
smile. Right eye shadowed by strands of dark hair.
Wise, cool, stable. She radiates an updraft that
stills the tornado churning at my core
with the promise of a heavy downpour.

Memory Care

There's nothing to remind her of who she is
or the life she led. Nothing to remind
her of home where sweet smells of
made from scratch cooking perfumed
her kitchen, or the murmur of wonder
sat cozy on the blue floral sofa when
she read *Make Way for Ducklings* to
grandchildren. There are no photos of
her wedding or her daughter's graduation.
No dimpled mahjong tiles to remind her
of friends and games they played.

Strangers help her to bathe and eat
and dress in clothing that's too big
or too tight. The intimacy confuses her.
After breakfast she sits in a wheelchair
fidgeting with a *Barbie* coloring book or
sounding out newspaper headlines that no
longer have meaning to her in a room where
country music videos play all day. Trivia
games and concerts and chair yoga are offered
to stimulate the mind and exercise the body
but she's too frightened or shy or insecure
to participate. Nobody encourages her to join.

At night she sleeps in a bed with rails.
Vivid dreams summon the crinkle
of taffeta, musk of jasmine, bite of lemon
ginger. When she becomes restless
they give her *Ativan* with a sip of water
to keep drifting shards of memory calm
until she melts into nothing at all.

Making Room

Already our home is a museum of cast-aways
and redundancies too precious for Goodwill.
Take the white Staffordshire dogs she says,
so we do.

Or the Grosz ink drawing,
legless specter on her bedroom wall.
I don't even know it's there,
so we bring it home too.

What do I need them for? she asks
about etched water glasses and
ornate covered serving dishes
before they migrate to my buffet
giving her cabinets room
to breathe.

But today when she says
Buy something that will remind you of me
I sense she has transcended,
from unburdening and bequeathing
to the realm of anticipation
where the purpose is to clear
a space in my heart
a waiting room ready
for my grief
when she is gone.

Uphill

When I pass the barren cornfield newly plowed
where bell-bottomed butternut squash rest sideways
scattered like corpses on a battlefield,
I pump and steer and pump some more
ignoring my wobbly knees,
panting lungs,
and fingertips gone numb
from a too tight grip on the handlebars.

Nowadays it takes mostly nerve,
faith in equilibrium,
and confidence that the truck so near
I can feel the breath of his engine
will brake when I steer clear
of potholes, broken glass
and lumps of roadkill
fragrant and swarming with flies,
smeared across both lanes of
the country road.

But it wasn't always like this.

When the training wheels came off
and I mastered backwards footbrakes
the world pulsed with possibility.
I could ride alone to the schoolyard
where packs of big kids smoked cigarettes
and threw rocks at rumbling trolley cars
and educate myself on how to be cool.

Or I could ride by myself to the square
park my bike in the metal rack
and wander the aisles of the pharmacy
before stopping in at Bob's
for a roll of *Lifesavers*
to stash in my pocket for safe keeping
during the pedal home.

Though it's never safe to look back
to check that the deep whistle trailing behind
is only the wind,
at this late hour,
I steady my eye on rolling terrain ahead
comforted still
in knowing how to downshift
for that last climb home.

May 28, 2019

My first selfie,
taken during
a private moment
between me
and my mortality.

Am I looking straight
ahead? Upward and
inward? Ready for
battle or assuming
defeat?

My face is framed by waves
of long gray hair.
Mother's hooded eyes,
hazel brown dark
puffy bags beneath.
Father's semitic nose.
Time's marionette lines
etched at the corners
of my mouth.

I am ready. Impatient
to awaken
groggy as Briar Rose
from a magical slumber
induced by
an elixir of IV drugs.

Changed. Armed
with knowledge.
Body bathed
with hope.

Ash Friday

I want to do it on Thanksgiving,
the day of his birth. It is mild
enough, wind low, but the logistics
are impossible so I settle for
the next flannel-gray day.

I launch with the wind at my back
and paddle past the inlet for side
creek. When I come to the split, I think
about Frost and choose my favorite
channel, the one to the far right.

Everything looks different this time
of year. Water lily overgrowth in the process
of decay broadens the channel. Submerged
stems, like thick spaghetti strands, strangle
my paddle. Bare branches wave skeletal
arms. No turtles bask in the sun.

Partially drowned limbs make an easy
to maneuver obstacle course. Flocks of
black dots flap in formation heavenward.
I sit a moment and close my eyes, resting
with the sway of the boat. All is quiet
except for the rustle of a woodland
creature padding over crackling leaves.

Once I've found the right spot, far enough
into the channel for privacy, but not
so close to the rapids where fishermen
congregate in season, I take from my pocket
the vial, no bigger than two thimbles
stacked one on the other.

It is filled with gray dust—all that remains
of you—all that will remain of all of us—
when time comes and passes,
as time must do.

In My Next Life

I want to live with the Dragon Nuns
of Nepal on a hill overlooking Katmandu.
I'm ready to shave my head. Swap leggings
and hoodies for prayer robes. Abandon
cell phone and pockets. Still my core
with morning meditation.

I vow to use an iPad solely for scrolling
The Pearl of Wisdom during devotions.
Offer my voice to a chorus of chants
in a whitewashed temple and walk
for months on a pilgrimage picking
up trash along the way.

When I join my warrior sisters
on the esplanade for plein air kung fu
I promise to keep my stomps and
round house kicks grounded, soaring
only when a choreography of whirling
cartwheels delivers me heavenward.

About the Author

Elise Chadwick has long been fascinated by our potential for transformation at the edges of life's precipices. She received a BA from Franklin & Marshall College and an MAT from Brown University. She taught English in Chappaqua, NY for 30 years. In her retirement, she spends her time in NYC and Hudson, NY, swimming, biking, and kayaking with her tireless husband Michael and watching her grandchildren grow as they scale their own precipices.

You can read more of her poetry at:
elisechadwick.com

www.ingramcontent.com/pod-product-compliance
Lightning Source LLC
Chambersburg PA
CBHW070942160426
43193CB00011B/1775